WAVES OF MADNESS, WATERS OF TRANQUILITY

BY
AARON MICHAEL SINAY

PublishAmerica
Baltimore

First printing

ISBN: 1-4137-4368-4
PUBLISHED BY PUBLISHAMERICA, LLLP
www.publishamerica.com
Baltimore

Printed in the United States of America

This book is dedicated to my editor, my dad.

You need passion for what you do,
for your work to come across as true…
to form.

Table of Contents

Waves of Madness, Waters of Tranquility   9
Art's Enchanting Way   10
Adrift I See   11
Ghost Ship   12
Damned, Den-mad   13
Sorrow   14
Destiny   15
Fortress   16
The Tunnel   17
Void   18
Potion   19
Fill of the Pill   20
Oh Sweet Drug   21
Getting High   22
Sea of Insanity   23
Sins   24
Wanderings   25
The Emptiness Within   26
What of Numbers?   27
The Quiet Mind Dreams   28
Bayshan   29
The Lone Drone   30
The Gentle Medium   31
Fear or Awe   32
A Non-existent Shadow   33
Bones of Wood   34
Raindrops Don't Dry   35
The Lonely Ichthyoid   36
Infectious Mood   37
Why   38
The Clown with the Frown   39

Nameless Enemy	40
Devious & "Mis-*chie*-vi-ous"	41
Feeble of the Mind	42
Pieces of Peace	43
View of Self	44
Shakings	45
Evolutions	46
If I Am Not	47
My Diary	48
No Outlet	49
Tohiwo, Tohema	50
Soul Mate	51
Tremble	52
If I Were	53
Many A Thing	54
A Dear, Deer Friend	55
Wild Dogs	57
Flighty Friends	58
A Bird in the Hand	59
Metamorphosis	60
Seasons	61
Misty Mornings	62
Nature's Bell	63
A Cavern	65
The Nurturer	66
Legacy of the Trees	67
Can You See	68
Felled Trees	69
Who Would Bring	71
My Biology	72
Recollections	73
The Face in the Mirror	74
Woodpile	75
A Hard Life	76
Tribute to Pop-pop	77

Reflection	78
Goodbye to the Past	79
Cobwebs	80
Angelic Hallucination	81
History & Me	82
As We Sleep	83
The Soothing Sound of Snoring	84
Slumber	85
What I Dreamt	86
Penance & Arrogance	87
Towers of Trouble	88
Illusion	89
Brother of Moses	90
Mission	91
Just Who Is This?	92
The Dawn of Time	93
Everflow	94
I Only Know	95
Crystalline Sky	96
One by Night, One by Day	97
Goldenpeak	98
World Consternation	99
My Immortal Soul	100
Much More	101
Upon My Throne	102
Naysayer	103
I Am God	104
Ramblings	105
Spofgo	106
Rude Awakening	107
Olwoor	108
"De-Scepter"	109
The Old King	110
A Princess From Athena	111
The Fallen God	112

False Lord	113
Falon	114
Falonite Kingdom	115
Beasts of War	116
Grim Reaper, Time Keeper	117
Shadows & Light	118
NiSe Technologies	119
To Be A Machine	121
Irowom	122
Newoor	123
Delusions	124
A Dichotomy	125

Waves of Madness, Waters of Tranquility

Waves of madness, waters of tranquility,
Random, strange thoughts, lost in liquidity.
As if dissolved in acid, they disappear.
Only through medication does the insanity become clear.
They cannot be silenced in liqueur, drugs or beer,
And they snatch up everything you hold dear.
Like a fire intense, they sear, they sear.
They float into mind like waves on the ocean surface,
With no correlation to gender or race,
Like rain droplets that sweep across the water in quiet rings,
As movement on a lake, nature, it sings.
A veil is pulled down over the brain,
And we are left isolated, and labeled insane.
With a vengeance it starts to drain,
And we, stripped of our intellect, are made plain.
Fresh taste of sweet lunacy, like sugar cane.

Art's Enchanting Way

Art has an enchanting way
Of making time melt away.
Visual and auditory cornucopias of stimulation,
Presented oft in cultural celebration.
It's in these realms that artists are born,
On their sleeves are their loves worn.
I fancy myself an artist too,
Composing words in such a manner for you.
Read my rhymes, ponder my times.
Decipher their meanings as watching mimes
Construct a tower of lingual harmony.
Find me in life, and give me company.
I'll paint pictures with words,
As throwing feed to the birds,
The brush is my pen on the page.
I've become another sage
Who has created works beyond my age.

Adrift I See

A body trembling from fear of the unknown,
As the seemingly eternal slumber of aberration has grown.
As we slip inside our heads, little progress is shown.
Spiraling down the center of a temporal cone,
Our deviant behavior, none will condone.
Lost am I, like a cat up a tree,
When an oar is lowered to steer the boat adrift at sea.
We are left to wonder who has saved us, man or God, and can we
possibly see?
Finally realizing who we can potentially be,
Am I the man who has treated my illness, or is the illness me?
Only when I answer these questions will I be free.
Now as I learned to swim in the waters, I swim through the expanse
of life.
The pain in my head cuts like a knife.
But through these tribulations I sail,
As a dolphin passing by a whale,
The whale is society and their leering eyes.
I am the one you have come to despise.
Do you not see how through these experiences I have grown wise?

Ghost Ship

Fog overwhelms the captain at the helm
Of this ship lost at sea, and we cannot see
That in order to be free,
We must drift even further from you, and me.
In the depths of the sea, as in the mind,
It's hard to ascertain and find,
And to feel at all in kind,
That we are not alone,
On this ship made of bones.
Bones of the trees, to float on the sea,
Below the deck is a speck of a treasure,
That was found for your pleasure.
This jewel is a tool, to be carried by a fool.
In school, there's a rule, not to duel,
With the teachers and the preachers
Who are the soul-seekers.
As are the shipmates.
Their beer mugs are beakers
For experiments, of late.
This ship is of ghosts who will boast
They've traveled the most, from coast to coast.
When you encounter them, your very soul will roast.

Damned, Den-mad

This is a ship of the damned, who are den-mad.
Mad of the den, known as a cabin—
Cabin of seven men,
Drawn to madness once again.
Each man is I, I who would die, to keep the prize.
Would he subtly lie, and wonder why you look with suspicious eyes?
They are bound to be sure I am mad at the core.
The ship is a metaphor for my mind's door.
The door goes to the base of this rat race.
When the ship was sunk, the men were drunk with power,
The world they scour, by the hour.
When this ship lands in port,
You need only report that I've become that unwanted sort.
I'm a pirate looting your valuables,
I'm scooting, with what's feasible,
To take not from your body or homes,
But from your very minds, where I now roam.
My ship sails in your head,
From the day you read my words, until you are dead.
It's a ship of mind control, and of your soul.
I've taken on the role of the Lord in whole.
This is a magic ship, which you cannot banish,
And just when you try to remove my influence it will vanish.

Sorrow

This disillusion has become like a dam bursting free.
My sorrow has drowned out my woeful plea.
I feel utterly alone and aimlessly adrift.
Searching for golden events, in the dirt I sift.
So tired of living, fatigued of being sad,
Taunted by voices and delusions, as if driven mad.
Unable to comprehend my brain's imbalance of chemicals,
Tormented by a mind gone hysterical,
Lost time slips away as I have shrunk in my bashful fears.
I experience such anguish, yet come no tears.
I want to go to heaven to be with the angels,
I hunger to be where God dwells.
Yet I live each day as it passes into the eternal realm.
I set sail on this vast ship, standing guard at its helm.
I take flight in my sleep, as a turtledove.
I dream of strange worlds, from lust to love.
Gone, the innocence of my youth.
Shed, the words of the uncouth.
Left is the remnant of my tortured mind,
Given a moment to ascertain and find
Pills to make me once again whole.
I wonder—are these marks of my body, or my soul?

Destiny

What am I, but a man destined to die,
Seeking religion for a spiritual high,
Dreaming at night I can fly,
Being sad and wondering why?
Medications with which I never cry,
I take a deep breath and sigh.
In life I am given to try
To live each day, content by the by.
The end is at hand, a handful of sand
In an hourglass, where time will pass;
I am but a creature full of energy and mass.
When my time comes to move on,
I will embrace it, and no one will know I am gone.

Fortress

You'll never enter this castle,
To grind with mortar and pestle,
The antidote, in the form of a note, that the King wrote,
To place you in a straightjacket, disguised as a coat.
Now you're crossing the moat,
Of the mess,
Of a fortress,
That stands in opposition to your advances
Of subtle dances, in pursuit of chances,
To acclimate to other's stances,
You're a prisoner of the court,
So you need only report,
To the dungeon,
For you are to be a carrier pigeon.

The Tunnel

At the end of the tunnel is a light.
It's the end of your life, and you must fight,
But it's just a bad dream you had tonight.
You woke up to find you're all right,
The light, so bright,
In opposition of night,
The tunnel is a metaphor,
For the part that is sure you will endure,
And be content, forevermore.
I've gone through tunnels before;
At the end is always an opening,
A dream of winning,
A new beginning.

Void

"I'll leave you with a void," he toyed.
I listened to his ramblings, and I was annoyed.
Just who was this demon, and how was he employed?
To whittle my days away,
Take from my fun, and not let me play?
Who was he to say that I would soon die, not far from this day?
Horns on his head? Nay.
"Fight or flight all the days of your life,
Be ye alone, and find ye not a wife."
He speaks with such guile,
And torments me all the while.
He takes pleasure that I am not free.
Am I too blind to see that the demon is me?
He's my shadow, stalking ever so viciously.
The shadow is but a metaphor,
For the part of me that's not alive anymore,
The part that died, deep down inside;
On the day I was born, God said I would be great,
And he lied.

Potion

The water has shrunk from an ocean,
To a potion, that induces an emotion.
An artificial relic, in the midst of an epic,
Of gargantuan proportions,
And you simply look
Through the lens of distortion,
At a clown in contortion,
Of your mirror image,
To gauge your wage,
As a sage, who can no longer turn the page.
The healer, is a dealer,
He is a Shaman, a humble man,
He'll make you whole,
But it'll take its toll,
On your soul.

Fill of the Pill

To be cured is my will,
For I've had my fill of the pill.
I recognize I am ill,
But it bothers me still,
To see I've no choice, or a voice,
To speak my mind, of my kind,
I'm emotionally distraught,
And mentally ill, as I'm taught,
On me was insanity brought,
Freedom I sought,
A pawn, that's gone, to be wrought,
My tidings have gone for naught.

Oh Sweet Drug

In truth, the one whom you saw was not burnt,
But a phoenix who arose from the ashes of what you weren't.
Oh, sweet drug,
You tempted me,
But I rarely gave in to my desires to be free.
I simply tried it for a passing phase,
When it was the craze.
And now, I neither get high, nor drunk,
And your allure, is as a skunk.
My mind is clear,
My strength is here, and
The *only* chemicals I ingest
Are those prescribed by my psychiatrist.
For a while you were my daydream;
Getting high, by this scheme.
They all thought that I was wrought
In the irons of intoxicants,
It runs, oh so scant.
The high fades, and you are left with nothing,
Nothing but the depression it will bring,
You wafted your scent my way, like incense.
It incensed me to be mad with more sense.
You've no pull on me now,
And I've left those in your grip somehow.

Getting High

I'm not certain why,
But every once in a while, I've gotten high.
I suppose I wanted to flee
My sadness and sorrow, you see.
Intoxicants in the form of smoke rings,
Rarely to see the trouble it brings.
I miss the buzz,
Just because,
It took me out of myself for a while,
But it took its toll, and it took my smile.
I saw even fewer happy days.
My true self faded away.
I experimented but a brief moment,
A few times a month, spent.
Am I still to lament
The brain cells that died in my soul?
It solidified my resolve to stay in control,
Blocked the neurotransmitter sites,
Made me sleepy at night,
To eat food as a vulture,
And disregard my culture.

Sea of Insanity

Can you be free, if you're adrift on the sea
Of total insanity,
A complete sense of lunacy?
The waves flow beneath the boat,
And you recite your delusions by rote,
Take to heart what I wrote.
Fish swim below as if to taunt,
At the land-lover, looking gaunt.
The fish are symbols,
Seamstresses with thimbles,
Who are quite nimble;
And drummers, who play the cymbal,
Bang their instruments to the sound of trouble.
You fall into the water, encased in a bubble,
And a mermaid saves you.
The mythological creatures are well to do;
Nonetheless none of this is true.

Sins

Never you mind what sins I did wrong;
They were but training for this moment all along.
I see others who forgive themselves and I am awed.
I beat myself up for past failures, as if scratching my skin until it is raw.
Stalked by folks who judged me ill,
To lose and confuse them had to be my will.
I was to die and again be born,
To rescue in resurrection the people forlorn,
To weave tales from religions to make my story,
Envision new narratives in form allegory;
Given rise by my imaginative eye,
One of help and remedy was this cry.
Languages melded as I wrote in an alphabet I devised,
Though fragments of other letters it comprised.
I wrote in this dialect in a notebook at home,
I wandered my town in an effort to roam.

Wanderings

Be it day or middle of night,
I went out, took to flight,
By car or foot I surely was lost,
The damage of car accidents and trespassing was the cost.
On train tracks I strayed,
Recalling childhood games I played,
I drove and walked with no conception of where to go,
Just vague recollections of places I know.
Wandering on foot, meandering in my car,
I traveled alone and entirely too far.

The Emptiness Within

Can I atone for my sins
To fill the emptiness within?
The overwhelming sadness begins.
The voices fade to the sound of a dropping pin.
Empty feelings inside—have I died?
So long ago were the times I cried.
I said I was fine, but I lied.
I heavily sighed, with no peace inside.
Am I just along for the ride?
I feel a failure, for everything I've tried.

What of Numbers?

If a minyan is ten,
Then what of a billion?
The dreams of a thousand men
Can be the nightmares of a million.
Visions of construction
Can bring about destruction,
If used in the wrong hands.
And hope can spill, as sand.
We toil, to foil the plots of man now,
To embroil, with oil, the sweat of our brow;
Drill in the earth to bring up wealth,
And rich entrepreneurs drink to health.
We take nothing when we die,
Beyond the pale of existence, and we cry,
To mourn the loss of you and I;
A dirge has become a lullaby.

The Quiet Mind Dreams

The quiet mind dreams, while the criminal mind schemes.
They both try to hide the fact they're coming apart at the seams.
They've quite a conundrum, it seems.
Where will they find peace once more
If they're driven to insanity at the core?
Pandora's Box is opened, at insanity's door.
Both minds lost in the waves by the shore,
Drowning their sorrows in habits, be they of physical pleasure,
Or of mental distractions, games for sure.
We know they'll never find their way home,
If we do nothing more than let their madness roam.
Go over their ramblings with a fine-toothed comb,
Encase their flighty thoughts in a geodesic dome.
Harness the potential of a giant in the body of a gnome.
Now we've opened the wound, there's no turning back,
Keep your distance, or they will attack.
Check them like the vegetables in the bottom of a sack.
Take them on a journey and don't forget what to pack.
We've got the rhythm, now I think *you've* got the knack.
This morsel is not a meal, but simply a snack.
Read on for a while, you'll get on my mind's track.

Bayshan

Ani bayshan, I am bashful,
Meek, and shy, but my personality is colorful.
A bible says the meek shall inherit the earth.
I believe that bible came from God's worth.
I raised my hand and voice in anger only when coerced or sick.
When I struck out at others, it was but a nick.
I keep to myself, ever careful not to incur wrath.
Rarely do I cross another's path.
Now don't take me wrong, I'm not timid,
I'm just quiet, and withdrawn, and hidden in my mind's pyramid.
You look; you'll see a gentle soul,
Who'd harm not a fly, I prefer to cajole.
I'll give you my heart and spirit, whole.
So please be my friend, if you be nice,
And a part of my good nature I will splice.
I've had few friends in my life, whom I've outgrown, anyway.
Just as well most of them have moved away.
I try to make new friends at every opportunity,
For I take pride and joy in each familiarity.
I've got friends of all ages, young, middle, and old,
And I prefer those more advanced in years than I, truth be told,
For they are mature, like me,
But in time I'll make more friends my own age, eventually.

The Lone Drone

The lone drone,
Destined to be alone,
Seeks to find
A place of his own.
He's a man who hides in the shadows of the mind.
At parties and festivities you'll seldom find him.
He's content to retreat to a corner seat.
Is he an enigma, a riddle to unravel?
His depression leaves him with a look disheveled,
It's as if his home had been totally leveled.
He wants, he desires to be accepted,
He recalls with sadness the times he was rejected.
Deep in the recesses of his thoughts,
Are the ropes of timidity, drawn taut.
Is this the lesson he sought?
Under the wings of angels was he brought.
Is he a robot to be programmed to behave in the manner you see fit?
You know he's not assembled from a kit,
So he'll just drift every day a bit,
Until he lays his head on the pillow,
And hope the headaches will go away with aspirin from the willow.

The Gentle Medium

I present for your examination
A man, of great fascination.
He's neither tall, nor short,
And has no heroic deeds to report.
You've heard of the gentle giant,
Quite mild, and compliant?
Well, here's the gentle medium,
He's full of metaphors and aphorisms.
This man's related to both you and me,
By way of close or distant family,
Charity is his calling, kindness his standard,
Rather shy and withdrawn, you might say wayward.
Slow to fight, but sad to say,
If you start one with him, he'll run away.
But he's so nice, you really can't hate,
So just be his friend, and you'll feel great.

Fear or Awe

Fear or awe, hand or paw,
I'm afraid to live, or of going wrong,
Even more so, petrified of success,
As if the pressure would sever me from the throngs.
I've known much failure due to my head,
Many a time went to sleep praying to die in bed.
My past haunts me like a banshee,
It wails every day, stalking me.
I try to move forward, but I'm held back,
Yet I feel in my heart I'm on the right track.
These words I speak, they are so true,
And I hope to bring understanding to you.
Do I have fear or awe of heaven?
Do I feel welcomed on the day of seven?
I pray to be pure of mind, and free
To cast off unclean thoughts, imprisoning me.
This is a question I cannot simply ask or answer,
And in life when faced with challenges you mustn't surrender.
I can only foresee the need to be bold,
So I trudge on ahead, not knowing what the future holds.

A Non-existent Shadow

I'm a shadow of a man who never existed.
My accomplishments will never be listed,
In a book, or computers, or on screen,
No one will know or even care what I mean.
I am just a passing ship, to sail and never return,
And in the depths of hell will my soul eternally burn.
On pins and needles do I turn,
My place in society I've yet to earn.
And it's my duty to learn,
To reproduce thoughts like the spores of a fern,
I am but a cyst that gives hives,
I neither exist, nor even imagine being alive.

Bones of Wood

Say what you will, my life has been good.
Do you mean to say I have bones of wood?
Eyes of stone, a mouth of fire,
Do you not like my tone, or how I conspire?
If I've these traits then surely the rains
Will wear my eyes, and drive me insane.
The waters will rot my bones,
My heart is of rock, and it moans.
I care not for your petty drones.
Your robots,
Who amuse me not,
Your pawns, a-swim, like prawns in the sea,
Your lawns, watered at dawn by fools like me,
Green on the surface, black underneath,
Circular and contrived, as a holiday wreath;
My blood boils in your presence,
Bespeaking my toils, and your lack of sense.
You have cursed me since day one,
And my rebellion has only just begun.

Raindrops Don't Dry

Tiny spots on my hands and feet,
Small bumps gently caress the hands of people I meet,
Like beads of sugar on dough, so sweet.
I search for the meaning they contain;
If like land, they are a rocky terrain.
Like small drops of water, they remind me of rain.
I keep thinking, "Raindrops don't dry,
They just soak in the ground or float on by."
I have this mark on my skin and don't know why.

The Lonely Ichthyoid

Scaly, bashful, and paranoid,
Here comes the lonely ichthyoid.
My skin is itchy and I'm annoyed.
Dry, oily, make up your mind—
A cure for you is quite hard to find.
Do they make fun? They're staring at me.
This scaly red skin is plain to see.
It's like being pricked with pins, on my stinging skin,
Try medications, herbs and vitamins.
Please don't stare, it's really mean,
And don't ask what's wrong with my skin or I'll turn green.
Will somebody love me despite these scales?
And not be disgusted as I scratch until it bleeds with my nails,
Know that the appearance of my skin is beyond my control,
And under this exterior lies a gentle soul.

Infectious Mood

Upon close inspection,
You'll find my skin full of infections.
I've boils, from my toils.
I'm a mister with fever blisters,
My fingernails get infected every couple of years,
It's enough to cause a weaker man tears.
I've tried antibiotics and herbs,
There aren't enough words
To describe my dismay, being ill every day.
I wash with antibacterial soaps,
As my skin remains the same I mope;
I struggle to cope; I'm at the end of my rope.
What girl will take me, with this aversion to society?
It's not my choice to create this voice,
But I'm afraid to be paid what I fear is my due,
The choice I have made is true,
I chose to be alone,
Ever since my infections were grown.

Why

Why was I even born, why do I feel so torn?
If you are given to scorn, should I just feel forlorn?
Judge me by my character today,
Not by my acts of yesterday.
I've a painful past that won't go away,
It's not for you to say, how I should play.
Couldn't I have stayed in heaven, to be spared this strife?
Why should I be a heathen, all of my life?
I was a thief stealing my own innocence,
Arrested by the authority of my own mind, and hence,
I gained a conscience, moved to a place of subtle salience.

The Clown with the Frown

I was the clown, wearing the frown;
Am I here to make you laugh?
I present silliness on your behalf,
To hide my sadness I make mirth,
I rehearse these jokes to prove my worth.
They laugh *at* me, not *with* me,
But I'm too blind to see,
For I pretend to be happy,
As they are made merry,
Blind to any semblance of sociability.
I failed to realize I need not impress,
Dark was my mood, and in dark clothes I dressed.
This is my crutch, to which I clutch,
Who I am, I know not how to show you,
When I feel alive my mind will be true.
I still rehearse my actions days beforehand,
Petrified of things not going as planned.
Though I'm not the clown now,
Un-furrowed in my brow,
What you see is what you get,
I am as real as can be, this you can bet.

Nameless Enemy

Perhaps this bully is afraid of me
Surpassing him in society.
I'm far smarter than he, and he can't see,
That someone in life I will be,
Whereas he'll be nothing in ten years,
Consumed by regret and fears,
Menial labor for his remedial mind,
Love of academia in him you'll not find.
He once hurt me with fisted hands,
I buried my angst listening to angry bands.
Why am I so mad at the world?
I blame him, for the contempt he hurled
My way, but today I'm strong for having survived these times,
I've made lemonade from lemons and limes.
I've forgiven you, but I'll never forget,
By this verse my revenge is set.
You won one battle, my onetime enemy,
But your nameless face will no longer taunt me.

Devious & "Mis-chie-vi-ous"

I deviously, and "mis-*chie*-vi-ously"
Desired to be free,
Free of the trappings of society
That dictate our personality.
The introvert within me
Works viciously and haphazardly
To stay away each day
from the extroverts, at play.
They seek to endow me today
with their conforming ways,
to no longer quietly say
everything I think of their group;
a dastardly troop, formed of primordial soup.
I follow my own ideas of behavior,
With a gentle demeanor, and a heart full of valor.

Feeble of the Mind

Do you not see, I bear ill will for your society
For how they have deemed me
Weak, feeble-minded, and unworthy?
In life, a remedial course,
To scream 'til I am hoarse,
Of injustice they've inflicted,
To see in their literature how I am depicted,
As a pariah, in search of a messiah,
Or as a complex of the mind,
To ascertain and find,
Just whom I've become.
Indeed, I've changed some,
From the impressionable youth,
Who would speak in a manner, uncouth,
To a man who's still bitter to the core,
And regretful about my past evermore.

Pieces of Peace

Forget about world peace, I'd just like peace of the mind,
But it seems this missing piece is not mine to find.
Perhaps it was ill defined.
From the depths of the conscience it is mined,
Drilled into my head, from the day of my birth,
For cosmic purposes was I bred, to carve a place on Earth.
I'm a puzzle waiting to be solved,
From a simple boy I evolved,
I've a knack to attack the naysayers in the back.
On the rack is a tack, holding up a little sack
Of spices that are nice, and enticing to mice,
But it's so high that they'll die trying to get to this prize,
Wonder why they did tie this trap to devise,
Is the mouse in your house as bad as a louse?
Take a drink 'til you are soused,
Because today you killed, on the soil you tilled,
A little creature…
Who was God in disguise,
Only you failed to recognize him,
In the vengeful thrust of your eyes.

View of Self

How do I redeem my self-esteem?
To become confident, and know I'm competent,
To accomplish in life, move past prior strife?
I look in the mirror, and frown,
As I recall when my life was turned upside down;
Down by a mental illness,
Crushed by the diagnosis.
Despite my successes I fear failure,
I wait for my mind to be made pure,
I wish to not be in despair anymore;
Beggars would ride, if wishes were horses.
Who gave me these grades in courses?
Surely they were rigged for my benefit.
I know I work hard, but I don't feel fit to be successful,
And happy about it.
Perhaps only after making sense of this mess
Will I ever feel I am worthy of goodness.

Shakings

I'm shaking as a leaf, with great relief,
Pass the barrier reef, to cast off my grief.
I shake and quake, for my own sake,
A comfort I take, that I'm awake.
Yet it's a dream, in the seam,
Of the time, with a mime,
The silence...
With patience...
Spoken by my conscience...
With subtle acquiescence.
Can I be relieved for what I've achieved?
Was it ever there for me to conceive?
Is the reality enough for me to believe?

Evolutions

Evolutions in the midst of a revolution, of thought,
Dilutions of a solution, desperately sought,
Reputations of consternation, was it for naught?
Devotions to a notion that can't be bought,
Oceans of emotion, by which we are taught,
In the end we send, messages in bottles,
It tends to depend, upon smoke signals,
With the sway
      of the play
            of the wind,
In the way
      of the day,
            we are pinned,
We may
      have to say,
         "We have sinned."
We meddle, with the needle, with thread,
And pedal endlessly in our heads.

If I Am Not

If I am not my illnesses, who can say what is me?
If I am a slave to my own fears, then what will set me free?
For a brief time I believed I was messiah, and then God by extrapolation,
I was to lead the seventy nations.
The delusions were a strange contradiction between my low self-esteem,
And a twisted God complex dream,
Am I God, no one could say?
Does it matter, anyway?
I know that when I get to heaven I'll be pure,
I'll worry not about my past anymore.

My Diary

My diary, what do you think of me?
Do I describe my experiences effectively?
Do I speak of my life eloquently?
Have I words of wisdom each day?
Will anyone care what I have to say?
Today I woke up and thought,
This is not the life I sought,
Why am I not dead?
I wish to go down to my grave, instead,
Sadness is my mood, sorrow, my food,
I nourish with self-deprecation,
Consumed by regret, and consternation,
I went about my current daily routine,
And had thoughts quite obscene,
I thought of ravaging a lady,
Exerting my will on her strongly,
Of hurting myself and others,
Of how I've disappointed my father and mother,
But they love me for who I be,
Faults and all you see,
Nonetheless I am alone, as always,
And feel as lonely, as a loner, all my days,
I am but a madman at play.

No Outlet

I dream of girls, and sex,
I've known not love, so this does perplex,
On me the females place a hex,
I admire them and then recall as I sleep,
The fantasies I keep,
Locked in the back of my mind for I am bayshan,
But can I help that I am a man?
So I will lie asleep,
And wish I needn't weep,
For the desires that have no outlet,
And hope one day, a girl I will get.

Tohiwo, Tohema

Lay me down on this woman,
Lay her down on this man.
I want to perform tohiwo,
To biblically know
This maiden, and grow.
She will perform tohema on me,
We'll fall in love, you see.
Intimate details will entail
This tale that sets sail,
From this port of loneliness,
To an island of happiness,
A place with a race
Of beautiful women, who hunger for men.
It's my dream, to scheme
Of a team, of me and a girl,
To finally be free and to give her a whirl.
Though I've dreamt of heaven above,
I haven't known love…
I've been alone all these years,
I've been drowned in my fears.
I sit by myself, watching love as an elf.
Time I spend at home,
Unaccompanied, alone,
Feeling small, and insignificant,
Inane, not fully cognizant—
One day though, tohiwo will come to pass,
And for her tohema, and gentle love will amass.

Soul Mate

Together, whoever she may be,
We would break the chains of war, and set the world free.
I thought we were Gods on earth in mortal forms,
To be resurrected to immortals, to challenge the norms.
She and I were to be wed.
We were already soul mates, as Adam and Eve, the humans we bred.
I knew not for certain her name,
Just to see her for the first time, or again to win this game.
We would build the house of the creators on the hill.
People would gather in a cave below, as time stood still.
They would ride on lions' backs,
With animals as companions, showing them the tracks.
An ape, an animal not quite man,
A parrot to talk as people can,
To visit when in distress,
When needing a parent to sort out the mess.

Tremble

I tremble in my boots as I search for the roots
Of my insanity,
With the certainty,
I am mad
Indeed;
I may never perpetuate my seed.
For why to bring such madness,
To the generation to follow,
Sow the seeds with gladness
That lunacy will be here tomorrow.
Nay, I'll just die alone,
As they bury my bones,
Who will read my tomes?
Who will hear my soul moan?
From below the ground, my own epitaph is my last sound.

If I Were

Am I a living man?
I escaped my fears and ran.
Should I grasp life with joy,
Knowing solitude and despair are my toys?
Self-isolation since I was a boy,
So few moments did I enjoy.
If I were dead, would I weep?
If only I could go to sleep,
And peacefully awaken,
To the greetings of heaven...
I've been denied love,
From Earth and above,
I wish no longer to live,
I've nothing for the world
To give.

Many A Thing

Yes, I've come to know many a thing,
Mostly from curiosity, and the searching it brings.
So I suppose I am aged beyond my years,
Slightly less bashful or withdrawn in fears.
Yes, I'm learned, ask me what you will,
But know my acquisition came via sorrow and the pill.
My opinions shift focus in a frequent way,
So I change my philosophies from day to day.
I'll debate politics of nature, crime and wars,
But my tide reorients, like shells shifting on the shore.
Never will I stop seeking to know more.
If I lived for today, took joy in what I do know,
Perhaps my self-esteem would grow.
Ever more I fixate on the past, and everything I can't do.
If you tell me I'm of great intellect, is it true?
Or did my random collage of thoughts simply fool you?
Well, take me as I am, I am as you see fit,
I'll try to demonstrate that I've come to believe in it.

A Dear, Deer Friend

A dear, deer friend was to be found in the woods,
Though I had set out to kill him, doing no good.
I walked into the forest of evergreens, given way to oak,
I knew not this deer's genius until he spoke.
Honeysuckle crept along the forest floor,
Until the dirt and tree bottoms could scarcely be seen anymore.
English Ivy was there as well,
With Lady Slipper Orchids in bloom, as if sprung by Tinkerbell.
Hollies to the left and right,
Dawn freshly arisen from night.
I saw the deer, and took a shot,
Went up to find the one I got.
A sharp piercing pain in my chest,
My heart sinks, as the bullet penetrates my vest.
I fall to the ground to find myself withdrawn,
Just then the deer scampers on.
I see a man, who walks up to me,
Places his hand on my chest, and heals the wound, magically.
He says, "It was I who intentionally shot at you.
I know now my aim was not true."
"Why?" I inquired, as I nervously perspired.
I lay down my head, shocked and tired,
Yet relieved momentarily I hadn't expired.
He said, "To teach you a lesson," as he transformed into a deer.
He continued to talk, though my mind was far from clear.
"Now the hunter is the hunted, and you know how it feels,
When you awaken from this dream it will still seem real."

I woke up to find I had tripped and fallen in a hole.
My gun had fired, out of control.
The hole in my vest and shirt was there, plain as day,
The blood was soaked in, but the wound had gone away.
I vowed never again to hunt for food, or sport,
And quietly said goodbye to my dear, deer friend in short.

Wild Dogs

Wolves in the woods will go after your goods,
Dogs in the house won't chase a mouse,
By your side they will sit,
Thinking nothing of it.
They'll raise your mood,
They'll beg for food,
With hunger ravenous,
bordering on *de*-vi-ous,
They'll chew upon your furniture,
in a manner most "mis-*chie*-vi-ous."
After a year or two they settle down,
Take them for walk, and it's their town.
Bark is the covering of the trees,
But for dogs it's the call of the wild, you see.
The dogs I've known, with whom I've grown,
Gentle companions, whose love was shown,
It was as if they said,
"Give me the pillow on your bed;
Give me water;
Grant me food and shelter,
In return I'll give you a lifetime of love."
Devotion like that comes only from above.

Flighty Friends

Birds in the sky,
Happier than I could ever be, you see,
For they are free,
Free to soar in the air,
On a wing and a prayer,
To do what most wouldn't dare.
Nonetheless they must beware
Of the ape without hair,
For he'll shoot them anywhere,
To put on his table for food,
Or up on the wall as a trophy for his brood.
What if that bird were to peck at *your* head,
And leave you for dead?
Would you instead have said,
"I'm sorry for threatening a poor flighty creature,
With angelic features?"
Admire their flight,
Watch them day and night,
For one day they may hunt you too, out of spite.

A Bird in the Hand

In the corner sits a man with a plan to hold a bird in hand,
But the bird, once held, quickly turns to sand.
Lost in shadows, still he is tan,
He took his thoughts and ran.
In his house, like a cat, he stares past the windowsill,
Now see him, on a hill, rocking back and forth, unable to sit still,
Trapped by the concept of free will; his hand holds a pill.
What is he, a beast at best, put to a test,
Filtered from the masses, then abandoned like the rest?
Time passes him by, and he leaves the nest.
Will he shed a tear?
Surpass his fears?
Keep on soul-searching 'til his destiny is clear?
The end may be near, and sadly he has no one to hold dear.

Metamorphosis

In the middle of June,
An insect emerges from a cocoon.
Soon to become a delicate butterfly,
It flutters by,
Beautiful to you and I,
Once a caterpillar, now a flying scholar,
And I on a book-leaf search for nectar.
For I have been a bookworm too,
Who took to wing and flew,
Perhaps I seem a nerd to you.
Took years to mastermind my plan,
To be a worldly man,
Flown over the seas,
An expanse he sees,
A metamorphosis of bodies,
Over land, over yonder,
A moment to ponder,
If I fly high enough, perhaps I'll reach heaven,
And they'll say, "We've been expecting you" then.

Seasons

You stand by a creek,
For peace you seek,
In the distance the trees creak,
And nature begins to speak.
You've visited this wood many a time,
Hied away home, covered in grime.
Wash away the dirt on your trousers and shirt.
In the garden where your vegetables grow,
Planting flowers, trees, and everything you know,
In the winter you've nothing to show,
But the roots of the plants are down below.
The barren branches are but a simple reminder
The plant's a lost object, and you, the finder.
You return it one day to nature and say,
"Thank you for your gift yesterday."
Once again in the wind the plants will sway,
Sowing their seeds, long after you've gone away.
Bulbs, dormant in the winter cold,
They've just gone asleep, truth be told,
In the spring they reawaken, despite being old.
Summer permits a brief sense of relief,
Winding down in fall, the plants provide peace,
Magically, like a golden fleece.

Misty Mornings

Heed my warnings of misty mornings;
A mist settles upon the lake, I go for a look, as I awake.
The water, glass;
The fog, a ship in passage.
I see the foggy mist today, walk towards it, still it stays.
I drive through the mist, and watch it percolate
Around my car, and it'll clear, if I just wait.
I'm enveloped by mist in the air.
It's as if God says, "Beware."
For the water is heavy everywhere,
I can't see ahead but I don't care,
For the mist is a gift from the sky, with coolness as its pair,
My mind is as foggy as the land is now,
The mist rolls in and out in but a few hours, and I don't know how.

Nature's Bell

Nature's bell tolls, as the thunder rolls,
Forces seemingly out of control,
Rains a-pummeling down, in sweeps,
Animals in the wild are awakened from sleep.
From a sheltered garage, I watch the thunderstorm bellow,
And recall watching with Viv, and feeling warm, and mellow,
While through our backyard a river would flow,
But only when the rains fell heavy, you know,
Whereas winter water falls as gentle snow;
Silently it drifts down absorbing the neighborhood ruckus,
And we'd go sledding, the bunch of us.
A white carpet blankets the ground down here,
Then the temperature rises, the snow and ice melts clear.
When in the spring, again comes the rain,
Bringing symphonic lights, with thunder and fountains.
It's a blissful mixture of sights and sounds,
The falling rain and the thunderous pounds.
Birds fly around, soaked in their feathers,
Dogs hide under tables, afraid of the weather.
I used to sleep like a log, right on through,
Now I awaken, to the noise of God's coo.
Mom and dad like to watch thunderstorms, too.
The clouds have a gathering, and meet in the sky,
The waters are voluminous way up high.
I feel at peace as the storms roll by,
Like God's brought forth water, just before his tears dry,
He cries because the land calls out for the water boy,

Not tears of sadness, but tears of joy.
When God reunites a soul with a loved one,
He cries a thousand tears of joy,
      As he briefly hides the sun.

A Cavern

A tunnel is a cavern,
And you a spelunker with a lantern,
A cavern is a recess in the earth,
A womb, and from it comes a birth
Of creatures, who were raindrops of mirth.
It goes on and on, seemingly forever,
To get to the end, it may be never,
But strive to get through, to endeavor
To improve, to grow, and be better;
You see it, a goal, to make you whole,
To complete your soul, put you back in control.
Cavemen lived many years ago,
And now, historians know
That they were the dawn of civilization,
Just as they ventured out in a collateralization,
And that mankind would survive the ice ages
To bring forth prophets, seers and sages.

The Nurturer

Each flower is as delicate
As a drop of water,
For it is but an offspring,
A plant's and God's daughter.
Intricate displays of colors and hues,
Shapes ranging from bells to shoes,
Central to the flower for the bird or bee,
Is its place of pollination, you see.
On the flowers, as they grow,
You'll find every color of the rainbow.
They wax, they wane, grow in fields on plains,
In the valleys, and in deserts, and on mountains.
And they drop their seeds to perpetuate their breed;
Flowers are but a reminder, that God is nurturing indeed.

Legacy of the Trees

The trees they are alive,
Into the ground their roots dive.
Born in the spring, in the summer they grow,
Have they knowledge, and what do they know?
Season of autumn, commonly referred to as fall,
The leaves begin to drop even as the branches grow tall.
I feel a terrible ache in my head;
Perhaps it is the sorrow of the trees, for their leaves are dead.
Full of such beauty and majesty,
Preserve them we must for future generations to see.

Can You See

Can you see the forest through the trees?
Do you see the busy bees,
On the flowers, pollinating happily?
Would you dance in the woods, at night,
If Mother Nature told you it was alright?
Or would you wait for the rising of the sun?
Could you tell the trees what you've done?
If man can't listen, or you dare not say,
Would you then say the whole truth today,
Knowing the trees won't betray your trust,
Ashes to ashes, dust to dust?
I've told the trees my deeds,
As they gave forth their seeds;
No, they won't talk in words you comprehend,
And you ought not hang on a branch on the mend.
Climb them if you will,
Plant one next to your windowsill.
Their wood is for building, though cut down just a few,
And don't forget to replant anew.
They'll bear fruit for you to eat,
Though their creaking isn't loud, it's their way to greet.
When you've no one else, talk to the trees,
You may be surprised how they can help you see.

Felled Trees

A Tupelo tree used to grow around me,
I'm a woodpecker you see, living happily
In the tall Tupelo, that had grown for my family.
There's a nest inside, where baby birds abide.
Then lumberjacks came to cut the Tupelo down, needing lumber for
the local town.
As the tree is tattered, their world is shattered.
I've a mind for revenge; my life hangs on a hinge.
I seek the help of the beaver, who would choose to be a man.
He is a cleaver, to those of his clan.
He turns into a human, in the form of my Shaman.
He cuts down a tree over the house of the head lumberjack,
And carefully plans his attack.
The lumberjack emerges, to the sound of funeral dirges
For this one who did shape-shift, giving me a gift.
I asked, "Why, Mr. Lumberjack, did you fell that tree, destroying the
home of my family?"
The Shaman turned into a beaver once more,
The lumberjack blinked his eyes to be sure.
The beaver said, "This was for all the little woodpeckers,
Made homeless by you home-wreckers."
The lumberjack thought he was drunk,
Thought he could smell a skunk.
So he went back inside the damaged house,
To go back to sleep, as quiet as a mouse;
His wife and kids yelled over the tree that was felled
To avenge the destruction of where the woodpeckers dwelled.

He glanced back outside and saw the woodpeckers glide
Smoothly past his home, as if taunting him like a gnome.
So the next day he set out to give them a new home.
He placed the woodpecker's nest and all in an oak,
Then he spoke, "This replaces the home that I broke."
The beaver scampered by, to say hi,
And all, including the lumberjack and woodpeckers, did cry.

Who Would Bring

Who would bring children into this world?
Children curled, in the fetal position,
An elemental composition, of thought
That was wrought,
And caught in the ebb
Of a web of a spider;
The spider is the government insider, inside her.
She is Mother Nature,
And nature is sure to spurn
Those who would seek to destroy,
With vicious ploy,
That which God created when he was a boy.
The world is his toy.
An ebb and flow will grow
As we come to know and show
That we are but mortals,
In search of a portal,
To another realm,
With God at the helm.

My Biology

Do not my shoes become muddy
In the rains of the biology of my body?
Cell divisions in mitosis,
Gametes formed of meiosis,
Chromosomes that are diploid go haploid,
Chemicals go out of control, and I'm left paranoid.
Amino acids, such as tyrosine in the brain,
A precursor to dopamine, that can make you insane,
If in excess, and obsessed with the inane,
I'm not phased by the phases,
They're just phrased, in genetic places.
Amino acids, in search of peptide bonds,
As ferns wave in the wind with fronds,
They spread their spores on the wind,
Yet we have to fornicate, for we have sinned.
A zygote formed of an egg and sperm,
That swam into the female as a worm,
A flagellum to swim, to the egg on the brim;
What went wrong with me?
Was it at fertilization, or a latter mutation?
For some reason I've too little serotonin,
Too much dopamine, and tyrosine;
Whatever else my biology may be,
I am a crucial part of my family tree.

Recollections

Memories given a space in time,
Words to flow, describe these moments in rhyme.
Time is lost to eternity, as day passes into night,
I can only hope that through my years I have done most things right.
Recollections of whom I used to be,
Pictures are the only true way for these lost epochs to see.
History books, movies, and the like,
Scrapbooks for laymen tell of the growth to a man from a tike.
Turn the pages, ask the sages
If they've learned enough through the passage of an era;
Here we move along on terra firma,
On earth each day, and recall,
Seasons pass from winter, to spring, summer, and fall.
Is it so bad to try to forget the pain,
but to relish the peaks, the joy and the inane?
If I could remember every day of my life,
I'd tell of the stories in pockets of merriment and strife.
No, not all of my days have been sad,
Nor have they been happy, but enough have been glad.
So I look back, and reflect,
And hope that heaven is a time machine
in which I can see my past and redirect.

The Face in the Mirror

When I look in the mirror I see a face of sorrow.
Yet I also see a dreamer, lost in the realm of yesterday and tomorrow.
As I look in the mirror my dad is there,
So long as I'll live, one face I'll share.
We are different, and as I get older I look more like him,
But we talk frequently, sometimes on a whim.
He is outgoing, and I am shy,
And I haven't figured out why.
Now I see, that he is me;
My face: past, present, and future, to be.

Woodpile

As I endeavor to be better,
I now realize, through my own eyes,
I am, indeed, building a little higher
The woodpile, as I aspire.
For in these words on the page,
I will be known as a sage.
It is, in my own way, to do today,
What I feel will surpass my father,
And please my mother.
Though I'll never have two college degrees,
I know they will always be proud of me.
Both my dad and I have a spiritual high,
Of composing, by the by;
Whether anyone will see in me, wisdom,
Is simply in the hands of the heavenly Kingdom.

A Hard Life

Pop-pop, every time we visit,
You always tell the stories of your life.
Moments in distant dreams that brought you to where you are today,
The folds of time float away like waves on the ocean.
As I listen to you drift back into your past,
You weave a pattern of a bygone time,
When you could walk from New York to Philly without a care in the world,
How a tough man was made of times of trouble,
And how you became wise and kind from a lifetime of stories.

Tribute to Pop-pop

I always admired you as a man self-made,
Even with hard-dealt cards, the game you still played.
Orphaned at twelve years,
No doubt consumed by fears.
Shifting from one family member to the next,
Educated by yourself at the library, delving into text.
Finally to find a career in furniture making,
Breaking out on your own at sixteen, with an apprenticeship undertaking.
Later to own a business alone,
A wife found, whose business prowess was shown.
You raised three lovely daughters, grandchildren to follow,
A guarantee of generations tomorrow.
I never grew tired of your stories of your past,
We formed a bond that would always last.
Now you've gone to heaven to be with Bubby Mary,
You may be served last, but God will not tarry.
You had a long life, at four score and eight,
I write this for you, as I think of you as late.
Your mezuzah, your rings I will wear with pride,
I hope in heaven above, peace unto you will abide.
Goodbye Pop-pop, until I see you again;
This is from your only grandson, Aaron, recalling the time with my Pop-pop, way back when.

Reflection

It seems I've dreamed beyond my means,
Thought of myself as a genius, playing among fools in fields of green.
Do I have apologies for deeds I've done?
Perhaps I should fly into the sun,
To be stripped of my conscience of this mortal form.
But do I not possess great fortitude and goodness, as the norm?
Am I not simply of flesh and blood,
A creature formed of God's breath and mud?
Do I have not a right to err in my ways,
To stray from the path, only to return most of my days?
If a dream of Utopia is enough to free the enslaved mind,
Then salvation is certainly mine to find.
Am I not simply a product of my environment?
Does not my bashful nature yield a gentle temperament?
I've yet to find my place in the present.

Goodbye to the Past

To reach my true potential, this I imagine,
To be out of the reach of harm once again;
Now I know I've sinned, and I've tried to repent,
But am I truly doomed each day to lament?
Now with these times gone, I move ahead.
I am pretty much content with my life, I could have said.
Yet still the voice begs, "Did you make it out alright?"
I suppose only those in heaven know, as I pass through day into night;
I reflect on the past, and move on forward,
Ever searching for my reward,
Goodbye to the past, the present is but a wink of an eye,
The future is now, as *that* moment passed by.

Cobwebs

In a gentle ebb and flow,
I clear the cobwebs, and know
A spider climbed through my mind;
A mess of junk he did find.
My mind is a polluted place,
You'll find it a convoluted space.
I've found my way each day, to say,
That I am smart anyway,
And stay to play, and dream away.
I've good grades to show,
That I can grow.
It's been a struggle, as if living in a bubble,
Of trouble, that has turned double;
In it I have made a stitch,
And I have found my niche.

Angelic Hallucination

I recall an hallucination of an angel,
Who took the form of my sister, to tell
Me not to hurt my mom,
On a day I wish had not come.
I was to try to harm with vicious intent,
And the time was almost spent.
I threw my mom down when she blocked my way
To the kitchen one day;
I was just caught skipping school,
And acted as a fool.
I saw Viv in the corner of my eye,
As I thought I was choking my mom while I was high.
I recited it from my memory,
Both of them said to me,
That is not what did occur,
My sister does concur,
It's interesting to note,
I never laid a hand upon her throat.
In fact, Viv wasn't even there,
Which is why she didn't care.
So I found redemption from an angelic creature,
Who presented herself with my sister's features.

History & Me

What will history know of me?
What will I leave behind for others to see?
My possessions, they do not suffice,
Though this would be nice.
I seek to impart wisdom,
If only to establish my own Kingdom;
King of the castle, commander of the fort,
Mortar and pestle, to prepare my sort;
Sort of food, to feed the seed,
Kind of mood, in need, indeed,
They'll see these words upon the page,
Perhaps it will become all the rage
To debate what was said by an obscure sage.
Nay, I'll be forgotten,
They'll think me rotten,
For what I've done in my own name;
They'll remember just the same
That I never sought fame…
Just honor and good deeds,
A scholar, of whom to read.

As We Sleep

What are dreams at night but mere reflections of our thoughts, in flight?
We drift along in our mind, as we sleep away,
Recalling and interpreting, abstractly, the moments of the day.
Memories sometimes intersperse,
In recurrent dreams, of shadow and verse.
Perhaps we find joy, and dream we can fly,
Or are lost in sorrow, and nightmares, and want to die.
Whatever it may be, dreams are strange, this is true,
They are simply the collection of what makes me and you.
Are they of mind or spirit as well?
It's hard to say, and no one can tell.

The Soothing Sound of Snoring

The soothing sound of snoring,
Like a kitten purring,
My dad snores in the other room,
I drift to sleep as the euphony looms,
The sound resembles the whistling of the wind,
Some might say we snore for we have sinned,
A cacophonic roar in the middle of the night,
Nay, a pleasant, pacific calming, all right,
Now say what you will it keeps you awake,
Why doesn't white noise make your bones quake?
Oh stop it, they say, for heaven's sake!
A lullaby without words,
A soliloquy of a dreamer, ever so slightly heard,
Rest, go schluffen, it's time for sleep,
Or as I once said as a child, "Now I'm gonna go to fleep."

Slumber

Some say heaven is a land of eternal slumber,
Where our soul takes time to remember.
I've had dreams of the past, present, and future,
Be these just memories and projections, or psychic I can't be sure.
For what is time but a circle, a Möbius strip that doesn't end?
Our dreams always have a message to send.
They are our fears, our hopes,
The sum of our imagination, that allows us to cope.
Whether you dream of angels, or devils,
Of hope that builds, or terror that levels,
Dreams are not what you have to see,
Just the possibilities of what might be.
So as we sleep take them to heart,
And know that dreams are a portal to another world set apart.

What I Dreamt

Yesterday I dreamt I was flying,
Today I dreamt I was dying,
I woke up in sweats, paying my debts,
To society, for my thoughts as they be.
I think of violence, of death,
In a subtle salience, of breath,
Where is my patience?
It lies underneath.
My conscience,
Unto you I bequeath.
I dream of being chased,
Of having my life erased,
From the sight of history,
I am but an enigma, you see.

Penance & Arrogance

An arrogant landscape was made,
Of many worlds, and stars of a grade,
Why should there be more than one?
Why should the sky even have the sun?
This act of arrogance grew of the penance,
Of the true God who left heaven for earth,
And got lost in human suffering and mirth.
He forgot he was God in the way of the land,
But not the angels who lent their hands;
They watched over him each day from a distance,
And endowed him with a conscience.
When he finally realized who he was,
They did rejoice, in a voice because,
God had returned to his seat,
Without ever to set his feet,
In the throne-room, and the power now looms.

Towers of Trouble

It was in primordial caves
That the earth did save
Man's soul as he sought shelter.
But he forgot this lesson and built a tower,
The Tower of Babel, today's skyscrapers.
The tower was meant to challenge heaven,
Led by Nimrod, the warrior heathen.
I see no difference between the Tower of Babel
And skyscrapers, boulders to a pebble.
Man erects gargantuan structures,
And thinks nothing of the damage incurred;
Damage to the environment,
Of no concern to the government.
A disaster, be it natural or manmade,
Will level these mammoths to the grade.
I'd like a simple structure of one floor,
Made of recycled products, door to door.
One day, I hope I'll be able to say,
I was humble in my dwelling,
And meek in my living.

Illusion

I don't know why, I must die,
To see through the lie,
That the devil has created, by the by,
Such as the myth of a solar system up high;
There is but Everflow, now known as earth.
You will soon know of its joy and mirth.
It's a terrarium, in essence,
That contains the Collective Conscience.
God for now is a collective like the Borg on Star Trek,
But the Collective's predecessor has a noose around his neck.
The noose is a metaphor,
For the part that isn't God anymore.

Brother of Moses

I have a plan, to be more than a man,
A dream comes to me, of late,
To be God, incarnate.
On Everflow I am to go,
To the house below,
Goldenpeak, and humbly show
To the people of the world what I know.
Brother of Moses, by my name,
I am Aaron, too, we are one and the same.
Reincarnated to life anew,
Centuries later I speak to you,
You made the golden calf,
And so Moses broke the tablets in half,
I made a golden mountain in myth,
Which shall stand as a monolith,
For now it is but on paper,
But it is a grand dream,
You must concur.

Mission

I thought myself a traveler through time,
A heavenly messenger of the sublime,
Determined to shape the world anew,
Set on a path straight and true.
The angels had already measured my worth,
I was to be the vessel of peace on earth.
I took moments to reflect on my past,
I found serenity in forgiving myself at last.
Back to creation's sixth day,
The mistakes of history were to fade away.
All killings made in the name of God, devil, or man,
Were to be erased from time in my master plan.
I was to bring a fresh world all my own,
Yet I could not recognize my delusional tone.

Just Who Is This?

Who is this God?
Why, he is me!
It took delusions of grandeur for me to see,
Prove I'm *not* God; why, send me to my grave.
I am foolish, and but a knave,
If you send me this route, I'll find all about
God sooner, rather than later.
My soul will be greater,
I'll settle for nothing less,
From all this, I stress,
When I die I will be God, incarnate,
And you will say, "Who was that madman of late?"

The Dawn of Time

In the dawn of time, in a land of grime,
God shaped the world as he saw fit,
In space and gently twirled it.
The scroll was then unfurled,
Of the history of the universe,
The creation was rather terse,
He created by shadow and verse.
The air was full of soot and dirt,
The animals were of a nature, curt.
Big creatures, these dinosaurs,
Who would disappear, forevermore,
Their existence overshadowed by man's wars.

Everflow

We are dreaming in the midst of a fiery ball,
The fury of which consumes us all.
This is the temporary domain of hell,
In which the devil and all of us do dwell.
God is but a man, who executed a plan,
To be humble, and meek;
He dreamt of creation the first day of the week.
I know this for I am that God indeed,
Though I've no supernatural powers or seed.
I have escaped in knowing who I be,
And one day I will reveal for all to see,
Dreams of Everflow, when I awaken,
I will stand in awe of my own creation…
Once again.

I Only Know

I only know, we live on this place,
An island called Everflow, floating in space;
You'll find no true pictures, or maps,
It's a land of chance, and mishaps.
The world we see now is an illusion,
Meant to be drawn by the devil for confusion.
At the drop of a hat, he will make a sound,
The world is not flat, nor is it round,
It's a purely circular island,
That has neither ocean around it, nor sand.
There are rivers, and lakes, but no seas,
This Everflow, you must be enlightened to see.
At the base of Goldenpeak,
Is the home you seek,
The home of God on Everflow,
And his wife, you know.
From Goldenpeak flows the Spofli River,
To the Purwat Lake, as a sliver.
Houses of stone, houses of brick,
For all the trees say, "We spare not a stick."
Call it heaven; call it paradise;
I call it Eden, given rise twice.

Crystalline Sky

I envision a crystalline sky,
Of silicon gas, frozen by the coldness of space up high.
A dome to cover the face of the Earth,
Spinning clockwise for gravity, and mirth.
One continent again, Pangaea rekindled,
And hope for the star that never dwindled.
An eternal light to shine, as Isaiah said, sevenfold,
Prophesied by this man of old;
The night to be as bright as day,
All creatures at night, to frolic and play.
Is God in heaven, why can't he be on earthen land?
He'll be here one day, approaching as the tide across sand.
An immortal being, never to die,
With an immortal wife, yet be they delicate as you and I.
Angels come down to join,
Reincarnated souls, as well, gently entwine.
A government of heaven formed of this holy gang,
As creation completes the big bang;
We touch the sky at the edge of the world,
And know we are alone in the universe, on this sphere that was
twirled.
Close up the seas, we need them no more,
Dry up the lakes, and rivers a bit, and widen the shore.
Stars in the sky there will be but one,
That is the light of our everlasting sun.

One by Night, One by Day

One by night, one by day,
To shine upon the folks at play;
Call one the sun, the other the moon,
Both reflect with passion upon the lagoon.
Each with its own name,
Do you not see they are one and the same?
The sun is a mountain called Goldenpeak,
In a place of which no one does speak,
It's a mountain of gold, to conduct the heat,
And God lives at the foot, in a heavenly seat,
The moon appears when the heat and light wane.
But in the new days it will be plain,
Plain to see, that the mountain is free,
Can it be, that Goldenpeak is before me?

Goldenpeak

In Maryland in a place no one has been before,
Is this Goldenpeak, this place I do adore.
At the foot is a door, though I scarcely see it anymore.
I've been there only in my dreams,
It's a place of my mad schemes.
The sun is not a star in the sky,
That star is but a reflection on glass way up high.
For the Goldenpeak is a summit here on earth,
Its existence coincides with my birth.
One day I'll climb it, and know the middle of the land,
The holy mountain is here, not in the sand.
To see it though you must know the truth,
I must be a soothsayer, for I speak the sooth.
See the sun for what it truly must be,
And you too will climb Goldenpeak with me.

World Consternation

I seek to achieve world consternation.
I have a deep sense of frustration.
I have an affliction, and I'm full of contradiction.
For I must see the sufferings of mankind,
I am ill of the mind,
And yes I am a bit schizophrenic,
You may say my ideas are pedantic.
I'm not a leader of politics,
My message is a matter of semantics.
But salvation is mine to find,
Am I the messiah,
perhaps more a pariah?
No, peace be up to you,
Only heaven knows if my path is true.

My Immortal Soul

What's that you say, you're worried today
About my immortal soul's destiny?
Don't you worry none about me.
My soul will be fine, as I draw the line.
Worry about the one called Adonai,
Who led me astray and I wonder why.
He must pay for his sins against mankind,
When I get to heaven this creature will be in a bind,
And my plan is nothing short of lunacy of the mind.
I'm the true God, humble, and meek.
The universe is in need of a tweak.
Perhaps I strike you as a geek,
Salvation is not quite what I seek.
Worry not your little head,
After all, I can't be judged until I'm dead.

Much More

Can we truly think that we'll never die if we attain a spiritual high?
What of religion, is it a carrier pigeon,
To heaven directly, to inject me with knowledge of eternity?
I hunger to never again know pain,
To not have to experience the drain
Of madness upon the brain,
And of the physical as well;
Life has become my hell,
The prison in which I dwell;
My mind is my own cell.
I dream of being the Lord,
Perhaps because I am bored,
Or better still to explain what I have endured,
At the core, I know for sure,
I am much more, than one knocking on heaven's door.

Upon My Throne

Ever since I was grown, I have known,
That I sit on my throne, all alone;
Can you condone, my tone?
Upon me countenance was shone,
I am a God, in the body of a man.
You may say slipshod, is my plan.
When I ascend to heaven then,
To become this God again,
I've a God-complex indeed,
It fulfills my need
To be in control, of my soul.

Naysayer

Enough with the prayers, I'm a bit of a naysayer.
They're driving me mad, and I'm feeling sad,
Sad that you can't see the truth,
Even as you stand in the booth,
And fight by the skin of your tooth.
This God you pray to, he is not true,
His magic and trickery have fooled you.
Why, the false God has let millions die unjustly,
While he sits in heaven, nonchalantly?
Would he really reward death for beliefs?
He has stolen his role, he's a common thief.
He is not God; he is but an angel, growing
In power as a wolf, in sheep's clothing,
I know who you are; you don't fool me by far.

I Am God

My life has been slipshod,
Until I realized I am God.
I came to earth to learn to be a man,
I took my thoughts and ran.
I am not just a mortal creature,
Kindness is my most beautiful feature.
I know I can never be the same,
After I make this claim,
And make holy my name.
I am humbled by this existence,
And have gained a righteous conscience.

Ramblings

Ramblings murmur from my lips,
Gambling on wine, with a sip,
That I'll not be drunken,
With visions of heaven;
If I inspect my own dialect,
I see I am mad indeed.
What madness issues from my seed?
A seed that has yet to be planted,
My views are rather slanted,
I do hope you will become enchanted,
With what I conceive;
My message you will receive,
In time you will believe,
That you were naïve,
To seek God for penance,
Even as you doubt my existence.

Spofgo

In truth Spofgo is the sooth,
The combination of every nation,
A compilation of a restoration
Of thought, and words,
From the serious to the absurd,
Every language spoken by God, and man,
English and Hebrew, are within its plan.
But each and every tongue
Lends a place upon the rung
Of the ladder, to heaven with the latter,
It should be a simple matter.
The closer we come to blurring the lines
Between tongues of men, then we become fine.
And see this was our language, all of the time,
With meter and rhyme,
The words I write day and night are part of my fight,
To restore the light, to Everflow, all right.

Rude Awakening

I've had a rude awakening,
From my dreams as I was sleeping;
Have I really woken up though?
I scarcely know.
I hear rumblings from below the great mountain of Everflow.
Where is this mountain, who can say?
I'll ascend it someday,
A chance to dream upon a scheme,
Inside the seam of the theme
Of time, with a mime,
Who tasted a lime and committed a crime.
He spoke when he was understood to play mute.
He wrote notes to play as a flute.
He took a chance with his life,
While the piper played the fife;
He talked of the Newoor,
And he was quite sure
That once they saw he was asleep no more,
On his very life they would close the door.

Olwoor

Long ago lived the Olwoor,
Though no one knows they exist anymore.
I am the last of my kind,
The truth I have defined,
My ideas I have refined,
To find within my mind,
The story of the people of Garofed,
Thought long since dead,
Those of the Garden of Eden,
Considered now to be heaven.
This is the Olwoor Code,
Presented in a restorative mode,
The old world order they be,
To be led always by me,
I am the first, before Yehovah,
My soul is as old as Methuselah.

"De-Scepter"

This is the dawn of a new chapter.
In my hand is the scepter,
But I am a defector, from the Kingdom of my predecessor.
He was a King in his own right,
But his Kingdom fell one night,
In the midst of a firefight,
A fight that might end tonight,
If I make it out alright.
I awoke in a space,
To find I was King in his place.
Was it a delusion, perhaps?
A series of mishaps,
My Kingdom lies not on the maps.

The Old King

I am King, and I am my own subject.
Silence, he will detect,
When the old King returns in the fire that burns;
But I am the man who would have his turn
To be King, if only I could learn
To control my own destiny, in the fragments of my history.
A scroll unrolls to tell of my soul.
The control…took its toll.
He returns from the hills of war
To see he is not King anymore,
Bellows he, from below the door,
Mellow am I, you know for sure;
I took his throne, and he is to settle the score.

A Princess From Athena

I forgot for a moment, my own precedent,
Caught up recalling my antecedent.
Who elected me president?
Was it for my detriment?
A source of lament,
For this would-be government,
A need to repent,
My mind has gone up for rent.
It is an open book, in a crowded nook,
That someone took, and I forsook.
Who made me leader of this place?
What gave me the will to finish this rat race?
Nay, I am but a former follower,
Who elected myself chief reformer.
The reforms of the norm,
The term of a worm,
In the bottom of a bottle of tequila,
Who fought the lions in the center of an arena—
Now I wait patiently to taste the pleasure of a princess from Athena.

The Fallen God

In the dawn of the age of man,
I formulated a plan
To construct a world of great beauty,
But I lost my powers as I forsook my duty.
Everflow was made so very long ago,
Garofed, its only nation,
Spofgo, its holy language in conversation;
Spofgo is the tongue prototypical,
Of the people prior to Babylon categorical;
In the city of man, called Siofma,
And in the city of Lords called Sioflo, we saw,
The original Olwoor, the creator,
There is none greater!
He is humble and meek,
Of the Olwoor tribe, he is the Sheik.
That creator is I, and once, I could not die,
But I sacrificed my powers to the Newoor,
For I was not sure,
I should rule anymore.

False Lord

Would you really trust your future, to a creature
Who made you so weak, as to speak of the "meek" you seek,
Yet remains outside your grip, as you slowly slip
Away from whom you are today?
Your organic body's natural composition
Will fail you in time of timely opposition.
If your heart's with Yehovah,
He'll let you rot; he'll rule with a fist while in absentia,
He'll drive you to madness, to dementia.
While you foolishly pray to be in heaven one day,
He'll take your loved ones away,
Let your foes smirk, as they play
On your fears and prey.
So as long as you believe in this false Lord,
Your chance for revelation will be obscured,
If "Vengeance is mine," sayeth the Lord,
I seek vengeance of my own accord.
For one day he won't be Lord anymore.
I will be restored to my throne,
As King, even if you'll not condone
My beliefs, and how I've grown.

Falon

I condemn you Falon,
For being the false one,
Your sinful deeds must be undone.
For me, the battle will be won,
As I send your soul into the sun.
You are called Adonai,
But your countenance is a lie.
Yehovah, you have no sway over me,
Your name is now Falon, you see,
And I have finally broken free
Of your iron grip, that drove me to insanity.
It's you that made me mentally ill,
It's you that makes me need a pill,
You made my skin blister in the summer,
You made my life a bummer,
You failed to avert bullies,
Kept me from the mountain, kept me down in the valleys.
Falon, you will fall, and on *me* they will call.
My life is mine to live, and mine to take away.
I decide what I give, and when I will die someday.
I know one day I'll be in Garofed as King,
And you, Falon, will be dead.

Falonite Kingdom

I can now see who the Newoor are,
The Falonite Kingdom, upon mankind a scar.
They've ruled for thousands of years,
Played on all of our fears,
They will fall alongside their Lord Falon,
The wind will pick up, and he will be gone.
He spoke to me as a child,
I behaved quite wild,
Before I came into my own,
For the true Lord, I had known,
Was indeed, me, myself and I.
It took me so long, by the by,
To find myself, and I almost had to die,
Though I know not why.
I died, in essence, as I gained a new conscience,
I must fight the Falonite Kingdom with the pen,
And wander into the lion's den.
The pen *is* mightier than the sword,
Especially in the hand of the true Lord.

Beasts of War

Iron beasts from land and sea,
Destroying all that they see,
Eagles with roars of lions from the sky,
Hail down their fury, for many to die;
Mothers lose children, and cry.
These are the machines of war,
Bows and arrows gave rise to more,
Guns and bombs, tanks and planes,
Ships with wrath, none can contain,
Nuclear weaponry, designed to deflect attacks on you and me,
Now built to show power in third world society.
Radioactive fallout, cancerous deaths,
Men on the battlefield take their last breaths.
Chemical and biological,
Weapons physical and psychological,
Traumas inflicted in the name of God and man,
One rogue leader unleashes his plan,
With each disaster of war, must we say never again?

Grim Reaper, Time Keeper

The living remember that death is somber.
I agree, but wrath rises within me,
That they are not here anymore;
I am not sure why they are gone forevermore.
Many wish to go down to dust, .
In life, yea, death is a must.
I wish to have life eternal,
Death stalks me, like a fire infernal.
Each day I grow weary, and bow my head,
Knowing in a few decades, I will be dead.
Perhaps I'll live to eighty-eight, as my grandpa did;
The shadows sought him too, but he hid.
Who knows when our number will be up,
When we can no longer fill our cup?
Grim reaper, timekeeper,
Mother Nature, can you escape her?
Both images take life down to the ground once more,
Where another existence opens the door.

Shadows & Light

Shadows upon the wall make their call, as we stand tall.
Light plays tricks on us all; the shadow *disappears* if we fall.
Stars grow bright at the sight of fright tonight.
Once, I was afraid of the dark,
But comforted by a spark
Of fire from a log on a pile
That reached up to the skies, all the while.
Ghosts and ghouls, hosts and fools,
Most people use their tools, boast of their schools,
I prefer the day, to play away,
I say, "What is your way, today?"
In the light of Goldenpeak's reflection,
On the crystalline sky is introspection.

NiSe Technologies

A reworking of the genetic code,
Will take place on the recombinant road.
Nanobots, produced by bacteria,
To replace the somatic cells in absentia;
The nucleus,
now a computer chip,
To reprogram the genes,
and skip

the genes at fault, bringing them to a halt;
Conversion of organic cells into inorganic ones,
like hair of nylon in lieu of keratin,
Liquid latex, for skin and blood,
In place of our feeble structure of mud;
Bones, eyes, and titanium teeth at the core,
Tendons and ligaments of steel ore;
Fingernails and toenails of metal as well,
Livers in which activated charcoal dwells;
Stomachs, intestines,
become machines and com-bines;
Hearts become muscles of rubber and steel
Mechanically meshing, to pump as a water wheel;
Brains of computers, and synthetic chemicals,
Nanobot Synthetogenics,
the mechanism for this all;
NiSe technologies, for short,
That can receive and generate a report,

With cellular phone capabilities in the nanobots,
All inorganic, synthetic bodies, that shall not rot,
A robotic, synthetic being, born of a former human,
I am capable of seeing I am to be that man.

To Be A Machine

A choice is in place, for my race,
To be human or robot, as commonplace.
If I had to choose between the two,
I would be a machine, wouldn't you?
For machines fail not their designs,
They think upon logical lines,
They can be programmed at will,
With no need of a pill,
To fix their malfunctions;
If I am to be a robot, I stand at the junction
Of the future and it's subtle commotion.
Though I'd opt not to be made this way
By surgery, or other invasive techniques today,
Instead NiSe technologies would fix me.
They would give me a code to call,
Nanobots in my body, and all,
The password AMSOL would control
The nanobots, but not my soul;
As I breathe, so too will they,
Spreading to the wind today,
And you too will join me, at last,
Leaving your feeble body to the past.

Irowom

The wombs of pregnant females
Will be replaced by rooms, in these tales,
tales of irowoms, in which embryos grow.
Where DNA will be the seeds we'll sow,
Like "Borg-ian" hives, for new human lives.

No longer will women be laid up to be pregnant,
No more will their days be stagnant
during this weak process of pregnancy.
You'll take to this idea. You'll see!

In the irowom we will culture factories of humans.
This will be the dawn of a new age of man,
Or rather the restoration of the Olwoor,
Who ruled once as machines, but no more.

Once, long ago,
Cells were nanobots, I know.
But Satan stole the world of old,
He took control and his evil did unfold.
Now I give you the Olwoor code,
To see technology and humanity as a converging road.

If you know not which to take,
Take them both, for my sake.
My next life will start in the first irowom you make.

Newoor

Never before have I seen the like of the Newoor.
They usurped those who rule no more.
They created a new world order,
From which it will be hard to recover.
In the first world there was but one Lord.
He ruled with kindness and endured.
But the evil inclination sometimes took his mind
As he struggled to find his place in the face of mankind.
So he set out to live on Everflow,
From a little knave he did grow.
His own true fate he did not know.
The Newoor tormented him so,
As they learned of his existence,
His rule fell through insouciance.

Delusions

The Newoor created illusions, manifesting delusions,
Fostering illnesses that bring on confusion.
Mentally ill, controlled by their will and pills,
A skin disease to make me scratch,
When I'm in the sun in a hot patch,
Or in the dead of winter,
Dry and cracked like a splinter.
Acid reflux to burn in my throat,
As crocodiles consume what falls in the moat.
Newoors have been efficient at war,
And they are evil to the core.
They've a book entitled, "The Code of the Newoor."
Beware, for they prey on unsuspecting souls.
I know they use doctors to conduct mind control.
If we fail to stop them they will take their toll.
Their greatest act, to form a pact
To destroy the original One,
As if his deeds were never done.
Nay, they will simply drive him mad,
Make his mood delusional, always sad.
I am he, who would be King once again,
But I need to let you see my ring, forged then,
That would identify *me*
As the true One, you see.

A Dichotomy

The soul in heaven is a dichotomy
Of good and evil, attempting to live in harmony.
The righteous cast off the evil soul,
Leaving the good one in control.
The evil inclination does remain,
And in time it will drain,
But some cast out the good instead.
Inside, these creatures are dead,
With thoughts of destruction in their heads.
Some even seek to reunite with the evil one.
That is when their troubles have just begun.
Even in the evil, a good inclination will stay,
But it's one that slowly fades away.
It's up to us to see the evil and root it out,
Not to let evil forces muck about.
Satan tempts those who would listen.
His lure holds steadfast, only in them.
Make no bones about it; they are not weak.
They are strong in their villainous ways, not meek.
Fortunate are the humble, for they rule the earth.
They are those who cast out the evil soul upon birth.